Jobs Around T

by Tammy Jones

4ELL00011544

Picture Words

 **chefs**

 **doctors**

 **firefighters**

 **police officers**

teachers

Sight Words

are

we

We are .

police officers

We are .

doctors

We are  .

firefighters

We are .

teachers

We are  .

chefs